QUICK PREP

Beginning the Estate Planning Process

What You Need to Know

ASPATORE

Mat #40883559

ISBN 978-0-314-90733-2

For corrections, updates, comments or any other inquiries please e-mail TLR.AspatoreEditorial@thomson.com.

First Printing, 2009
10 9 8 7 6 5 4 3 2 1

Praise for *Inside the Minds*

"Need-to-read inside information and analysis that will improve your bottom line—the best source in the business." – Daniel J. Moore, Member, Harris Beach LLP

"The *Inside the Minds* series is a valuable probe into the thoughts, perspectives, and techniques of accomplished professionals…" – Chuck Birenbaum, Partner, Thelen Reid & Priest

"Aspatore has tapped into a goldmine of knowledge and expertise ignored by other publishing houses." – Jack Barsky, Managing Director, Information Technology and CIO, ConEdison Solutions

"Unlike any other publisher—actual authors that are on the front lines of what is happening in industry." – Paul A. Sellers, Executive Director, National Sales, Fleet and Remarketing, Hyundai Motor America

"A snapshot of everything you need…" – Charles Koob, Co-Head of Litigation Department, Simpson Thacher & Bartlet

"Everything good books should be—honest, informative, inspiring, and incredibly well written." – Patti D. Hill, President, BlabberMouth PR

"Great information for both novices and experts." – Patrick Ennis, Partner, ARCH Venture Partners

"A rare peek behind the curtains and into the minds of the industry's best." – Brandon Baum, Partner, Cooley Godward

"Intensely personal, practical advice from seasoned deal-makers." – Mary Ann Jorgenson, Coordinator of Business Practice Area, Squire, Sanders & Dempsey

"Great practical advice and thoughtful insights." – Mark Gruhin, Partner, Schmeltzer, Aptaker & Shepard PC

"Reading about real-world strategies from real working people beats the typical business book hands down." – Andrew Ceccon, CMO, OnlineBenefits Inc.

"Books of this publisher are syntheses of actual experiences of real-life, hands-on, front-line leaders—no academic or theoretical nonsense here. Comprehensive, tightly organized, yet nonetheless motivational!" – Lac V. Tran, Senior Vice President, CIO, and Associate Dean, Rush University Medical Center

"Aspatore is unlike other publishers…books feature cutting-edge information provided by top executives working on the front lines of an industry." – Debra Reisenthel, President and CEO, Novasys Medical Inc.

ASPATORE

www.Aspatore.com

Aspatore Books, a Thomson Reuters business, is the largest and most exclusive publisher of C-level executives (CEO, CFO, CTO, CMO, partner) from the world's most respected companies and law firms. Aspatore annually publishes a select group of C-level executives from the Global 1,000, top 250 law firms (partners and chairs), and other leading companies of all sizes. C-Level Business Intelligence™, as conceptualized and developed by Aspatore Books, provides professionals of all levels with proven business intelligence from industry insiders—direct and unfiltered insight from those who know it best—as opposed to third-party accounts offered by unknown authors and analysts. Aspatore Books is committed to publishing an innovative line of business and legal books, those which lay forth principles and offer insights that, when employed, can have a direct financial impact on the reader's business objectives, whatever they may be. In essence, Aspatore publishes critical tools—need-to-read as opposed to nice-to-read books—for all business professionals.

Contents

The Importance of Client Engagement throughout the Process

Matthew J. Howard

Tax Partner

Moore Ingram Johnson & Steele LLP

ASPATORE

There are many reasons why clients seek to prepare an estate plan. The death of a loved one, the birth of a child, or an extended international trip all bring an individual's mortality into question. When that occurs, the individual realizes they need to take steps to deal with the transfer of their wealth upon their demise. The start of the process can never be too late, but there is no substitute for the benefit of time.

While the process can be complex, there are some basic issues about which an estate attorney should be well versed to ensure that the estate planning process is satisfying to the client: helping clients understand the process, preparing for the first meeting, keeping clients motivated and engaged, and common client misconceptions about the process.

When Clients Should Start Estate Planning

The specific timing depends on the individual, but there is no substitute for having plenty of time to plan. For example, most individuals with sizeable wealth—whether married or unmarried—should consider immediate estate planning. If a young athlete is making quite a bit of money, he or she needs to think about where that wealth ought to go and plan for it, rather than dying intestate (without a will or revocable living trust). If a fourteen-year-old tennis star is making several million dollars a year and dies unexpectedly intestate, that wealth goes to mom, dad, and siblings under most states' intestacy laws. If mom and dad already have a taxable estate, the last thing they need is more wealth being piled onto it. The federal government then gets more tax revenue from this family when the parents die. Therefore, leaving the wealth in trust will protect some of it from the government and direct it tax-free. We do not think of a fourteen-year-old as needing a will, but with earnings from a professional sport of millions, they really need to do some estate planning.

The First Client Meeting

The first meeting is a no-charge consultation. I see it as an opportunity to enter into a dialogue with the client, get them feeling comfortable with the firm, and have them meet the key players on the team who will be preparing their estate plan. I will have one of the younger attorneys in the meeting who will be responsible for the drafting of recommended documents so the client can meet them. That gives all of us the opportunity to talk about the current state of the law, and ask the client questions about their wealth and what it comprises, such as real property or liquid assets. We also learn about their objectives of lifetime wealth enjoyment and their objectives for when they pass away.

The client may have a specific idea of how this will all occur, but no situation is ever the same. It is essential for me to really get to know them as best as I can before we dive into the process. At the end of the first meeting, I try to reconcile their desire for lifetime wealth enjoyment with their objectives for distributing their wealth. Armed with that information, I can provide them with a roadmap—broad, of course—because we are starting at the top of a funnel and working our way down. We provide them a roadmap of what they can expect regarding document implementation and the associated costs.

Keeping Clients Motivated and Engaged

I am very candid with a client right from the outset. The more engaged they are in the process and with the team, the better their estate planning process will be. At the initial consultation, we have a standard summation statement. We tell the clients that they can hire us right on the spot, they can go home and think about it and then call us, or they can go home and never speak to us again. We do not take their home address or contact information. If and when they are motivated to complete their estate planning, they will engage us.

When they do hire us, we start the process by encouraging them to make it a priority and, in turn, we are quick to get discussion drafts prepared. The expeditious nature of our early work and the generation of discussion drafts are critical. Individuals believe estate planning is something they need to do both for financial reasons and for preservation of wealth. The reality for estate planners is that we cannot expect that the client will come to the table with great enthusiasm, ready to tackle their estate planning in a proactive, collaborative way. If we want an engaged client, we must be prepared to do a lot of coaching, hand-holding, and prodding. We are acting in our client's best interest. Even though it gets tedious at times keeping clients motivated, the outcome will be positive for the client and their descendants.

Counteracting Client Attrition

If a client is going to drop out of the estate planning process, it is going to be at the execution stage. We will invite the clients back to review the initial drafts of the documents we believe they should implement. Early in the process, clients are pretty good at getting us the information we need, such as deeds and financial statements and a detailed picture of their financial worth. Where the process tends to bog down is when lingering issues arise, such as guardians for young children and successor trustees for the assets once they are both deceased. The best course of action is to invite the client to come in and bounce some ideas around instead of struggling silently with the issue. We almost always arrive at a solution, because when they introduce an impartial third-party opinion, they get some clarity about resolving the issue.

The Most Common Client Misconception

The most common client misconception we encounter is their belief that they have to come up with perfect estate planning decisions. There is a misconception that the will they execute is set in stone, but the fact is that no will is effective until death. Of course, some trusts and documents are irrevocable, so we never want to discount the gravity of the discussion and decisions that are made. In the end, there is no such thing as perfection.

In estate planning, the attorney and client are trying to predict the future. We are discussing and planning for something that could happen twenty-four hours from now or twenty-five years from now. We are trying to predict the best person to leave in charge of this wealth many years from now. It's not practical to expect to come up with the perfect answer, but if we work together with the client, we can develop the best answer possible today with the full knowledge that the plan can be changed down the road. When we get past that hurdle, the process goes more smoothly.

Matthew J. Howard joined Moore Ingram Johnson & Steele LLP in 1989 and currently serves as senior partner in the firm's Corporate, Tax, and Estate Planning Department. Mr. Howard specializes in estate planning and has served as an active member of the Estate and Gift Tax Committee of the American Bar Association Tax Section since 1996. He has developed an expertise in the Small Captive Insurance area. In addition, he heads up the firm's Tax Litigation Department, handling disputes for individuals and corporations before the Internal Revenue Service, as well as litigating against the Commissioner of Internal Revenue Service in the United States Tax Court and the Department of Justice in United States District Court. Mr. Howard also oversees the firm's larger merger and acquisition transactions.

Born in Columbus, Ohio, Mr. Howard was admitted to the Georgia Bar in 1989 after receiving his economics degree from Vanderbilt University in 1984, and his J.D. from Capital University Law School in Columbus, Ohio. Mr. Howard transferred to Emory University Law School to complete his third year of law school and to obtain his master's degree (LL.M.) in taxation in addition to his law degree.

Making the Most of an Uncomfortable Process

Morton L. Price

Partner

Cowan, Liebowitz & Latman PC

ASPATORE

When Clients Seek an Estate Planner

Younger clients tend to think about estate planning after the death of a parent, particularly the second parent, when they start acknowledging their own mortality. Significant changes in a client's financial resources can trigger planning, as can the birth of a child since parents may wish to select guardians and establish a trust for their young children, in the event that both parents die.

It is never too early to start estate planning, but most people avoid the subject. If an individual has a minor child, estate planning is extremely important because money left without a will to such a child creates all types of problems. The assets will be subject to court supervision, and the guardian may need court permission to provide access to funds for other than the child's basic needs.

Client Misconceptions

There is no question that estate planning and considering one's eventual death is not a pleasant subject, so people find something better to think about or do with their time. The thought of having to make decisions about their estate, or how to treat people close to them, causes procrastination. Another reason is lingering misconceptions on the part of the client. We do our best to dispel as many of those misconceptions at the first meeting as possible, but there are so many notions about wills and estate planning and death engrained in our psyches that they can be difficult to overcome.

For example, many people think life insurance is not taxable, or that a spouse can be cut out of a will. In fact, the opposite is true in both instances. A spouse is entitled to a certain percentage of the estate unless that individual has waived that right, most likely in a prenuptial or post-nuptial agreement. Some people have serious misconceptions about what happens when you do not have a will (e.g., how money or property is divided among heirs). Another common misconception is that parents must leave money to their children. That is usually not required.

Parents are customarily advised to treat all children equally unless compelling circumstances dictate otherwise. A client can, of course, make an unequal distribution, but doing so can generate hard feelings and invite a challenge to the will. Moreover, disparities in children's financial circumstances can disappear, as has been too amply demonstrated by events resulting from the current downturn.

Ill-Advised Client Ideas

Sometimes clients will propose ideas or strategies that are not viable from a legal or ethical perspective. In those instances, the attorney should explain the potential consequences. The best approach is to work through the errant idea and propose an alternative, but sometimes there are situations in which the client will insist on having it "their way." Estate attorneys occasionally write wills and create testamentary estate plans with which they do not agree. If the document is something that can open the attorney to disciplinary complaints or malpractice charges, it is best to document the objections and the preferred approach in a letter to the client or, at a minimum, with a memorandum to the file.

Often, when clients see objections in writing, they retreat and modify their directions to us. If they do not, the file memorandum is a useful thing to have if the client later forgets that those were the instructions. Since there can be a significant gap in time between the first client meeting when you prepare the documents and when the client dies, sometimes many years, the client will forget why something was done in a particular way. When it turns out that the approach does not make sense, the client or family can be quite critical and confrontational. The documentation enables the attorney to remind the client or, subsequent to the client's death, the family, of the reason for the approach, and then, if possible, take actions to ameliorate the effects of the long-forgotten directions.

Collaboration with Other Professionals

Estate attorneys often work with other professionals when helping clients create their estate plans. Accountants, financial planners, and life insurance specialists are common members of the estate planning team. If a client is dealing with difficult family issues, a psychologist or psychiatrist can often help. The biggest challenges come when working with a husband and wife who may have totally different ideas or different estate plans due to prior marriages. If there are children from different marriages or if spouses have different views of estate distribution, it may, at times, be necessary to inform the clients that you can only represent one of them.

Even though "splitting" representation is the right thing to do from a legal, ethical, and strategic perspective, most people do not like the idea because they are not enthusiastic about what they perceive as additional cost for seeing two professionals for the same services. But without waivers from the clients, representing both spouses can be very awkward. It is very important to get consent from both parties to discuss anything they individually tell you. Many parents do not want their children to know about their estate planning. In such situations, the children will find out the details after the parents are gone, which often creates additional problems. However, many parents feel that it is not their children's place to know about the estate plan while they are developing it. Of course, an estate attorney must check with the client before discussing anything with the children, another professional, or any third party.

Challenges Working with Elderly Clients

If one child or other potential beneficiary accompanies an elderly parent to the estate planning meetings and, subsequently, that child or individual is favored in the will, that child or beneficiary may be exposed to a claim of undue influence. On the other hand, if you ask the child to wait in another room, the situation can become awkward. You nevertheless should do it. Where there is only one child, it will not create a problem because he or she most likely will be presumed to acquire the entire estate. However, if there are two or more children and one is not being treated as well as the others, it is important to ensure that you are not a party to what may be asserted to be undue influence. At a minimum, a conference with the client, alone, to ensure that the will is what he or she really wants is essential. Ascertain the client's reasons for preferring one child over the other, and memorialize the conversation in a memorandum.

Review of Estate Plans

Depending on the circumstances, the client should review their estate plan a minimum of every four to five years, even if it is a relatively simple review. Major changes in the estate tax laws (particularly at the federal level), changes at the state level, maturing children who go in different directions, and marriage and subsequent grandchildren are events that should cause clients to start rethinking their testamentary plans.

Selecting Guardians for Children

Selection of a guardian is often a difficult challenge, since parents often do not see eye to eye on the individual favored by one of them. For example, the wife may say, "I want my sister as the guardian." The husband may not like the sister, or brother-in-law, so the situation becomes complicated. Frequent review of the choice of guardian is essential. The appropriateness of the selection can be affected by a change in the guardian's health, marital status, finances, or location of principal residence, among other reasons.

Relinquishing Control

There are various ways to save money in estate planning, but these methods often require relinquishing control of assets. Where clients have more than adequate assets, considerable tax savings can be achieved by making lifetime gifts. However, it is human nature to want to control everything until the last possible moment. The client has to weigh not giving up control against ultimately saving money on taxes.

Naming children or others as co-trustees of a "bypass" or "credit shelter" trust and enabling them to outvote the surviving spouse on certain issues is one part of a strategy that can keep assets out of a surviving spouse's estate. Notwithstanding that the surviving spouse may receive all of the income from the trust and can ask for an invasion, they are often heard to say, "I want total control over all the money, I want to be able to use it when and if I want it, and I do not want anyone, particularly my children, to tell me I cannot access it." That stance will lead to unnecessary estate taxes when the survivor dies. Unfortunately, many people are just uncomfortable with the possibility of not having complete control of their finances.

Morton L. Price, a partner at Cowan, Liebowitz & Latman PC, concentrates his practice on estate planning, administration, and litigation, as well as real estate investment. He also advises start-up and privately held businesses in a variety of industries. Mr. Price brings to his estate planning and business practice expertise in succession planning for family-owned businesses.

Mr. Price is a member of the New York Bar. He attended Yale Law School (LL.B.) and Bowdoin College (B.A., cum laude, Phi Beta Kappa).

Key Considerations for Working with New Clients and Families

Dan C. Peare
Chair, Trusts and Estates Practice Group
Hinkle Elkouri Law Firm LLC

ASPATORE

When a typical client arrives for the initial consultation, he or she may have received word-of-mouth information from similarly situated individuals and friends, business associates or partners, neighbors, professional advisers (e.g., financial planners, life insurance professionals, stock brokers, accountants), and other individuals in their social circles. A few clients may have consulted commercial resources such as books or a newsletter from a professional in the area on selected estate planning topics in preparation for their meeting to discuss developing their estate plan. However, a client may also come to an initial meeting with no background of the knowledge or elements of an estate plan.

In general, a client's existing knowledge of the estate planning process is vague and elementary. Often, materials are misleading or misunderstood by the client. It is common for an attorney to inform a client of the basics of estate planning, such as the difference between a will and a trust, and the different taxes that apply to estates. For example, the federal estate tax currently applies to only those estates that have a gross value exceeding $3.5 million.

Client Motivation

Individuals are motivated by different factors or events such as life events, non-life events, and business factors. Life events often include the recent death of a family member or friend, severe illness, divorce, or the birth of a family member. Non-life events may include large changes in an individual's net worth, changes in tax law, or other legal changes that create new opportunities or prohibit past techniques, particularly those that are publicized and discussed in the media. Business factors may also motivate a client to plan. These factors can include the buying or selling of a business, entrepreneurial changes, the need to develop a succession plan for a closely held business, or the change in ownership of a business.

Common Client Misconceptions

Most clients do not understand the utility, purpose, or limitations of a will. Additionally, most clients do not understand that the death benefit of a life insurance policy is subject to estate tax if not owned properly. Finally, most

New York State Bar Association (Family Law Section: served as the youngest ever chairman; delegate to the House of Delegates; member, Executive Committee); American College of Family Trial Lawyers (diplomat); American Academy of Matrimonial Lawyers (fellow; served as member, board of managers, New York Chapter, 1989 to 1992); Association of the Bar of the City of New York, Committee on Matrimonial Law (1978 to 1982); American Bar Association; and International Academy of Matrimonial Lawyers (Founding Fellow, member, Board of Governors, 2000 to 2005).

Mr. Bronstein received an A.B., cum laude, from Harvard College in 1965 and a J.D. from the University of Virginia School of Law in 1968.

Divorce Preparation—Making the Best of a Difficult Situation

Judith E. Siegel-Baum

Partner

WolfBlock LLP

ASPATORE

Preparation and Proceedings

There are basically four ways a divorce occurs in New York. The two spouses each hire a lawyer; net worth statements are exchanged; negotiations are conducted; they enter a separation agreement or stipulation of settlement; they agree on grounds, file uncontested papers, and are divorced. That is the easy and simple way. In the process, there may be some valuations of property or a business or license or law practice, but the case is settled without any court intervention except to submit uncontested papers for divorce.

The second way is to serve a summons with notice for divorce on the defendant, who hires a lawyer. The matter is negotiated; financials and net worth statements are exchanged; and the case is settled, as stated above.

In the third way, the action for divorce is commenced with a summons with notice for divorce and a motion or order to show cause requesting temporary relief, i.e., support, exclusive occupancy, temporary custody, and visitation. A decision is rendered, and a scheduling order for discovery and trial is established. Rather than going to trial and expending huge funds, the parties settle.

The final way to get divorced is trial. There are major discovery issues and experts appointed by the court to value businesses and personal property, to appraise anything that exists. Then, if the parties are dissatisfied with the court appraiser, each hires his or her own appraisers, and the case goes to trial. A case like that usually takes one or two years to go to trial; then, after waiting for the decision, it may well be appealed.

To prepare for divorce proceedings, the client has to provide all the financials, beginning with prior tax returns. If there were assets that were separate property at the time of the marriage, they must be traced. The same holds true with pensions and retirement funds. It is easy if people use Quicken, but otherwise, this information must be reconstructed. Sometimes there can be a problem with lost records, which then require tracing. Banks do not keep records for more than five years. Generally, records can be rebuilt if the sources are out there. If clients worked at different places, the designations. The second phase includes more complex planning, including the use of irrevocable trusts and business entities.

Phase one planning is typically a thirty-day process. The key tasks include meeting with the client, drafting documents and sending them to the client for review, and meeting with the client to review and sign the prepared documents. This timeline can be shortened depending on the client's life events, such as death-bed planning, impending surgery, or upcoming vacation. Phase two planning, such as developing a gift plan with an irrevocable trust, can take anywhere from thirty to ninety days. With more complex plans, the process may take between sixty days and six months.

Reviewing Preliminary Documents

Attorneys and financial planners should ask for preliminary information that will help shape the estate plan; this typically includes the following:

- A family tree (including names and birth dates of family members), which is critical for identifying potential heirs
- A personal financial statement, which provides a snapshot of the individual's net worth
- The cash value and death benefit amount of all life insurance policies
- The ownership of the client's assets (his, hers, or theirs), individually, jointly, and tenants in common
- A list of business entities, including the identity of other owners and any stock or franchisee restrictions
- An explanation of how market value was determined for hard-to-value assets
- Any other estate planning documents or beneficiary designations impacting the estate

These documents are usually generated by the client or his or her team of financial advisers. If a client has recently applied for a loan, this same information will already be prepared for and useful for the estate planner in advising the client. The previously listed documents represent a basic starting point for analysis and evaluation by the estate planner. If the client does not bring this information to the initial meeting, the estate planner must obtain this information either orally or at the next meeting.

Using a Checklist

The personal information and preliminary documents used for the first meeting are a good starting point for an attorney to build a checklist beginning the planning process. If a client forgets to provide the attorney with information regarding all of the client's assets, the estate plan may or may not be accurate. However, the impact on the accuracy and completeness of an estate plan depends upon the materiality of the omitted information. For example, a forgotten checking account with $5,000 is less material and less harmful to the overall estate plan than forgotten out-of-state oil and gas interests or an expected large inheritance that is near fruition. A checklist can help clients identify all material and relevant assets they may have or reasonably expect to receive in the near future. The accuracy of asset values provided by the client from the checklist is not as important as is the client ensuring that all information on all material assets have been provided to the attorney.

Determining Assets to Include in the Estate Plan

Setting Long-Term Financial Goals as Part of the Estate Plan

Long-term goal setting should start with taking care of the client, and then focus on taking care of a client's beneficiaries. The estate or wealth shifting plan should not adversely affect the client's standard of living. To accomplish these two competing long-term goals, the estate planner must establish a "hierarchy of needs" with the client as a guide for planning. For example, a client should evaluate the amount of assets they need to continue their standard of living, provide the opportunity to travel or fund hobbies after retirement, and reduce their potential estate tax exposure now and in the future. Expected returns and investment plan performance can be modeled, providing an expectation about what the asset values will be in the future based on expected growth rates and yields. Future value projections should be limited to ten years in duration or risk obsolescence.

Evaluating Asset Availability and Liquidity

Documents that are helpful to identify assets are previous years' tax returns, personal financial statements, and income/expense information on business entities. Additionally, the client's expected asset yields and growth rates will help frame the long-term estate planning goals.

A critical step in estate planning is to identify the liquidity of the potential estate. Business assets, often a substantial part of a client's estate, are illiquid and difficult to transfer. Forced transfers during an administration phase can significantly reduce the value of business assets. Personal assets are typically non-income-producing assets, and therefore may be a drain on the liquidity needs of the estate. Additionally, personal use assets are more likely to have a higher sentimental value, but may not have a high economic value. Family conflict is often present with tangible personal property. The existence of assets in the following asset groups should be considered as part of estate planning:

- Liquid wealth, such as bank accounts, brokerage accounts, and life insurance
- Business assets, including sole proprietorships, partnerships, corporations, limited liability companies, joint ventures, and investment real estate
- Personal use assets, such as homes, cars, boats, planes, toys, and jewelry
- A catch-all category that includes assets that do not fit the above categories

During the planning process, only the approximate values of a client's assets are necessary. However, exact values are important and necessary for lifetime transfers and transfers at death. Often, the value of a hard-to-value asset must be determined by a qualified expert who provides a written, professional opinion.

Determining Estate Planning Options

Estate planning options may disappear because of a client's lack of testamentary or contractual capacity. Some options become unavailable because the client is on his or her death bed and there is insufficient time to implement a comprehensive plan. Certain business restrictions may limit the client's estate planning options (e.g., S corporation restrictions or franchise agreements). Occasionally, religious beliefs may also prohibit estate planning options.

Dan C. Peare chairs the Trusts and Estates Practice Group at Hinkle Elkouri Law Firm LLC. Under his leadership, the trusts and estates practice has expanded to be one of the top estate planning practices in Kansas. Mr. Peare has extensive experience in high net worth estate planning, asset protection planning, and planning with family businesses. Mr. Peare also assists clients with business valuations, charitable planning, and planning with life insurance. He has assisted hundreds of business owners, farmers, and ranchers in the preservation and succession of their businesses.

Mr. Peare has made numerous presentations relating to trusts, estate planning, and business succession planning on the local and regional levels. He has also had numerous articles published in support of this practice area.

Mr. Peare was named to Worth *magazine's 2008 Top 100 Attorneys, making him the first in the state of Kansas to earn the distinction. He has been recognized by* Best Lawyers in America *and* Kansas/Missouri Super Lawyers. *He is also active in the local, state, and national bar associations.*

Providing Effective Client Guidance

Tracy Adler Craig

Partner and Chair, Trusts and Estates Practice Group

Mirick, O'Connell, DeMallie & Lougee LLP

ASPATORE

I approach estate planning as a collaborative and interactive process between the clients and the attorney. My goal is to discover everything I can about my clients' family and financial situation so that I can help them achieve their goals and objectives in the most strategic, effective manner possible. For many clients, these objectives often include ensuring that their assets will pass to their intended beneficiaries in a tax-effective way. However, for some clients, even if very wealthy, other issues take precedence over tax savings. It is the estate planner's job to understand these objectives when creating the plan. Additionally, as clients often perceive estate planning as a very complicated process, I try to take a holistic approach: keep the clients focused on their goals, lead them through the process, and stay practical and goal-oriented.

Client Triggers for Estate Planning

Typically, I find that people begin to think about estate planning when they have children. While some people begin the process during the pregnancy, many begin thinking about estate planning much later. Generally, when clients are in their mid to late thirties, I find that they begin to realize they should have an estate plan. Other triggers that cause people to begin looking into estate planning include receiving a medical diagnosis, a death in the family, or hearing of an acquaintance who faces a devastating illness.

Dealing with Clients' Preconceived Strategies

Clients sometimes enter into the estate planning process with preconceived ideas about what they need for an estate plan. Often, I find that a client hears of a specific technique from a colleague, family member, friend, or sometimes the media. Many times, while well intentioned, the strategy is simply not appropriate for the client's specific situation.

While some attorneys will set up the initial meeting and deal with any misaligned strategies when the first meeting occurs, I prefer to have an initial conversation with the client prior to setting up a meeting. This phone call often tells me if my practice or approach may not be a good fit for that prospective client. I think this initial phone call is extremely beneficial, because neither party has to waste time with an inappropriate fit. If the prospective client is thinking one thing, and I am thinking something else, spending an hour together would not be advantageous for either party.

The Estate Planning Process: An Overview

After a short initial phone call with the client to obtain some basic information about their situation, goals, and expectations, and to discuss general costs, I suggest a face-to-face meeting. Initially, some prospective clients may approach me with an e-mail to ask about cost because of the perception that this is the most efficient way. However, I find that a personal conversation is essential to begin building the relationship and to discuss initial issues. The conversation helps frame both the process and cost. If the client is interested in going forward, I send them an estate planning questionnaire (usually via e-mail) and we set up an appointment. If the client is married, I ask that the spouse attend the meeting as well. About 95 percent of the time, the spouse will attend the meeting. However, there are occasions when the client will indicate that the spouse is not interested in attending or the client does not want me to represent the spouse.

The initial meeting can last anywhere from one and a half to three hours, depending on the complexity of the situation. I begin each meeting by reviewing the completed estate planning questionnaire with the clients. The questionnaire is an approximately ten-page document that the client completes and brings to the meeting. It asks for basic information regarding the client, spouse, children, family members, parents, and siblings, along with all asset information, such as real estate holdings, retirement accounts, life insurance, and so on.

After we review the questionnaire, I ask the clients if they have any questions or specific concerns. However, I usually find that reviewing the questionnaire and asking questions along the way brings most issues to light. I then discuss an overview of existing federal and state estate tax law. This discussion helps the clients understand if they are affected by estate taxes, and it helps them understand if more complex estate planning is necessary. The next segment of the meeting is a discussion about which property passes through a will (probate property) and which property passes by other means, such as beneficiary designation (i.e., non-probate property). Unless a person has been previously involved with an administration of a deceased friend's or relative's estate, I find that most people do not understand probate or how property passes when a person dies.

We then discuss the critically important documents that comprise an estate plan. In Massachusetts, these documents include both health care proxies (for medical decisions) and durable powers of attorney (for financial matters) as part of planning for incapacity. We also discuss if the client has a homestead declaration, which generally exempts the first $500,000 in equity of a primary residence from most creditors. (The use of such a declaration is very state-specific, and some jurisdictions may not use this document.) We then discuss the necessity of wills and trusts—what they are, why they are important, and the role they play in the estate plan. I encourage this discussion to be interactive so the clients will ask questions and feel more comfortable with the documents I recommend for them.

Finally, we review the decisions that need to be made so that their estate plan can be drafted, such as the selection of fiduciaries, trust structures, and ages for children to receive property outright. During this phase of the meeting, I also answer any final questions. Clients who need additional time to make these decisions leave the meeting with a list of decisions to make and information to provide (which I refer to as their "homework") so the documents can be drafted. It is my general practice not to draft documents until the clients have provided all of the necessary information. I find this is the most efficient way to draft, and it cuts down on the amount of subsequent changes that will be necessary. Generally, e-mail is the best method to convey the outstanding answers.

At the close of the meeting, I review asset ownership structure and beneficiary designation issues with the clients. If the creation of trusts affects who should be named in beneficiary designations of retirement accounts and life insurance policies, clients receive additional homework to obtain change of beneficiary designation forms. (These forms can then be completed and signed after the estate planning documents are signed.) Finally, I review fees and expectations about the timeframe to complete the planning process. Clients are then sent home to reflect on what they have be resolved outside of the Court, he or she will often recommend or even require mediation.

Collaborative law is a relatively recent phenomenon. In a collaborative divorce, each spouse is represented by his or her attorney. However, since a collaborative divorce is specifically geared toward avoiding litigation, everyone involved must sign a participation agreement stating that, should the collaborative process fail, the attorneys and other professionals involved in the case cannot represent the parties in litigation. The fear of having to start the process anew with different professionals, as well as the financial implications of such a scenario, often serves as a powerful motivator for parties to work through their differences to settle the matter.

Other professionals who may be involved in a collaborative divorce include mental health professionals, who assist the spouses as divorce coaches or child specialists, and accountants, or finance specialists, as they are called in collaborative law, to assist the parties and the attorneys in resolving the financial aspects of the case. Under the collaborative model, the case gets resolved almost entirely through negotiations conducted in so-called "four-way meetings." These are meetings attended by both spouses and their attorneys.

Litigation is a divorce action in court, where you present your case to the judge through your testimony, the testimony of other witnesses, and exhibits, and the judge decides all of the issues for you. Of course, this is generally the most expensive method of resolving a divorce case; it usually takes the longest; and the spouses give up control over the outcome. Litigation should always be your last resort. Unfortunately, sometimes there is just no avoiding litigation. It takes *both* parties acting with some good faith and at least being somewhat reasonable to reach an agreement. If one of the spouses is utterly unreasonable or is motivated solely by anger and the need for revenge, then, unfortunately, it's not surprising that the case may end up in court.

A Roadmap to a Litigated Divorce Case

If a litigated or contested divorce is your client's only option, it is necessary to provide the client with a roadmap of what to expect at every step of the way, and with a sense of the timeline you are looking at in your particular county.

You should explain that a contested divorce case begins when one spouse files a Summons and Verified Complaint with the Supreme Court and that there is a filing fee that must be paid at the time the Summons and Complaint are filed. Since the Complaint sets out the plaintiff's grounds for divorce and asks the court to enter a Judgment of Divorce, you should be prepared and gather the necessary marital background from your client to allow you to draft a proper Verified Complaint.

Once we are retained, our first assignment to our clients usually requires them to prepare a detailed marital history for us. We emphasize that we will use the marital history to prepare the Verified Complaint. We ask them to provide us with a narrative detailing their marriage, with specific emphasis on incidents that support their particular ground for divorce, whether it is cruel and inhuman treatment, actual abandonment, constructive abandonment, imprisonment, or adultery.

Once the Summons and Complaint are filed, they must be served on your client's spouse. At that point, the spouse is required to file a response within a prescribed period of time. This written response is called a Verified Answer. In it, the defendant responds to the allegations in the plaintiff's Complaint. If the defendant also wants to sue the plaintiff for divorce, the responsive pleading is called a Verified Answer and Counterclaim. In it, the defendant not only responds to the allegations in the Complaint, but also sets forth his or her grounds for divorce and the relief requested from the court. It is important that your client be aware of the possibility of a Counterclaim and to have him or her be emotionally prepared to deal with harsh allegations and to respond with a Verified Reply.

The next step in proceeding with a contested divorce is for the attorney for one of the parties to file with the court a document that is known as a Request for Judicial Intervention. In response, the court will direct the parties and their attorneys to appear in court for the preliminary conference. At that time, the parties each file with the court and exchange with each other one of the most important documents they will prepare during the divorce, the Statement of Net Worth.

The Statement of Net Worth is a document that sets forth in detail the parties' monthly household expenses, their income, their assets, and their liabilities. It is a comprehensive document and is required by the New York Domestic Relations Law to be completed by every litigant in a divorce action. The Statement of Net Worth gives the court a clear understanding of the couple's financial situation.

At the preliminary conference the judge will determine which issues remain unresolved in the case. The main issues that can arise in a case are fault (grounds for divorce), custody and visitation of the children, child support, spousal maintenance, and equitable distribution.

Also at the preliminary conference the judge will appoint an attorney for the children, and, to the extent necessary, one or more neutral experts. These neutral experts can include a forensic evaluator, who is a mental health professional, to do an evaluation of the family for purposes of custody and visitation; a business valuator if there is a business or professional license to be valued; and a real property appraiser to value the parties' real property assets.

Sometimes it becomes necessary to file a motion with the court requesting certain relief while the case is pending. For example, issues regarding payment of temporary support, payment of attorneys' fees, exclusive use and possession of the marital residence, temporary custody or visitation, or the dissipation of marital assets may need to be brought to the judge's attention immediately. These are known as *pendente lite* motions (meaning motions brought during the pendency of the litigation). If your client needs to file such motions, they should be prepared to file sworn affidavits based on the facts of their particular case in support of their *pendente lite* motions.

The next step in the process is for the lawyers to conduct what is called *discovery*.

Discovery is the legal process that lawyers use to gather information from the opposing side. We must obtain and review certain information regarding the assets, income, debts, and expenses to be able to resolve a divorce case. Your client may be able to provide you with some of the information that is needed. But often we need to make certain requests for information from our client's spouse, or we may subpoena information from other sources (such as banks, accountants, credit card companies, and the like).

The discovery phase usually concludes with *examinations before trial*, or, as they are more commonly known, *depositions*. At depositions, the parties, and sometimes third parties, are questioned about aspects of the case by the opposing attorney. The person deposed is placed under oath, and the testimony is taken down by a certified court reporter. We always explain to our client that the purpose of deposition is twofold: to obtain information and to freeze testimony. It is therefore crucial to make sure that your client is well-prepared for his or her deposition and that he or she knows to carefully listen to the questions asked.

Once discovery is complete, you have to prepare the case for trial. In our office trial preparation is a rigorous task. Essentially, we spend countless hours preparing the visual aids and court exhibits that we will admit into evidence at trial; we prepare our clients for testimony so that they know what to expect at trial; and we make sure that we interview and prepare any witnesses we may need to call to testify in support of our client's claims. On the appointed day, we move forward with the trial. At that time the judge hears evidence from both sides and then renders a Decision and Order regarding custody, property division, child support, and spousal maintenance.

A Further Word on Financial Discovery in Divorce

We encourage our clients to gather as much financial information as they can prior to the commencement of a divorce action, so as to provide us with a clear picture of the family's finances before the case even gets started. One of the primary functions of the divorce process is to make a division of the assets and debts of the marriage. To propose a fair division, we must know what there is to divide.

Unfortunately, documents and some assets have a nasty habit of disappearing as soon as a divorce action is commenced. Therefore, it is usually a good idea to ask your client to gather crucial documents to prove any separate property claim he or she may have and to prepare an inventory

Understanding Client Concerns and Goals Early in the Planning Process

Daniel R. Stogsdill

Partner

Cline, Williams, Wright, Johnson & Oldfather LLP

ASPATORE

Preliminary Client Meetings

The obvious reason why many clients first seek assistance with wealth transfer planning is a change in family circumstances (e.g., marriage, divorce, or starting a family). This is most often the case with clients who have more modest means of $5 million or under. Clients who have larger amounts of property and assets are often fairly sophisticated in this area. They have read the *Wall Street Journal* and *Barron's*, and they have been told repeatedly that wealth transfer is as important as wealth accumulation. Therefore, they will call us to figure out ways to pass their wealth on to the next generation in the most tax-efficient way.

When a client first visits us, we give them a packet that discusses general wealth transfer planning techniques we would possibly propose to them—strategies to achieve creditor protection and pass property from one generation to the next in tax-efficient ways, and strategies that can minimize family squabbles and dissension. If the client owns a business that involves employee stock ownership plans and they want to get out without current capital gain taxation implications, we will give them information about how probate and revocable trusts work, as well as information about health care directives, durable powers, corporate fiduciaries, and the use of consultants.

Charitable planning is a big part of our strategies for many clients with higher wealth amounts. Therefore, we will discuss how private foundation rules work, and we will explore alternatives to private foundations, such as community foundations and donor-advised funds. In some cases, we will look at whether a public charity might be appropriate for a client and then look at the various ways to maintain those entities if the client chooses to establish them.

Early in the process, we use extensive questionnaires to identify some of the client's goals, wishes, and philosophies in this area. We also need to obtain a complete history of the client's assets, current planning strategies, prior transfers and tax returns, possible inheritances, any estate planning relating to other family members that they can share with us, and business information if they are operating a small business.

We will then discuss various options that might be available to the client in terms of wealth transfer planning, such as what kinds of trusts they might use, and how their strategies might play out, depending on whether they decide to terminate the trust at a certain age rather than allowing the benefits of a trust to carry forward to the next generation. Fiduciary selection is a big part of a wealth transfer plan, and it is important to consider whether a certain state, other than the state where the client currently lives, would be a more appropriate place to establish their trust. For example, we may want to look at states where there is no income tax on fiduciaries or individuals, or one of the states that offer creditor protection for self-settled trusts, such as Alaska, South Dakota, or Nevada.

Spending Time with the Client

By the time we have gathered sufficient information through our extensive and fairly exhaustive questionnaire and personally met with the client, we usually have the information we need to set up an effective wealth transfer plan. Over time, we have learned to ask the right questions. As is the case in the medical community, understanding the client's family history is very important in estate planning, and there is no substitute for spending the time it takes to obtain that information.

It may take several hours in that first meeting to begin to know the client and some of their philosophies, and it is then important to try to open the client's eyes to their estate planning opportunities and options. Many times, clients will tell you about goals they want to achieve, and explain certain strategies in relation to those wealth transfer goals, not realizing that their current planning does not reflect the fact that there are many other options for solving their problems, or they may discover that there are problems they did not think of in relation to their estate planning.

Therefore, taking the time to obtain a good client history, and getting to know the client and understand them as a family unit, is invaluable. Often one question will lead to another, and you just need to follow a line of inquiry where it takes you. Indeed, sometimes seemingly irrelevant questions can help important issues float to the surface.

Working with the Client's Other Advisers

Wealth transfer planning requires a team approach, as we are not experts in every area that may affect the client's wealth transfer issues. Therefore, it is often important to bring in the client's financial advisers, such as any registered investment advisers or brokers who may be managing the client's assets, and if the client has an accountant who is preparing their tax returns, we want to hear from them as well.

It is important that someone play the quarterback role in the wealth transfer planning process, a role that we traditionally play. However, in some situations, the client may have a very close relationship with another adviser in the financial or tax realm, or a close friend they are reliant upon for advice because they trust their judgment, and that person could become the quarterback. Whatever the case, it is critically important that someone take on the role of coordinating the other advisers, seeking their input, and making sure the job gets done in the end. You need one person to take on the overall responsibility for the project.

Client Misconceptions about Wealth Transfer Planning

I have found that clients often have a great aversion to the use of corporate fiduciaries in wealth transfer planning. Indeed, the fiduciary's role in the process has often been the number-one complaint among my clients. Many of my clients had heard bad things about fiduciaries (e.g., that they are controlling, and that they charge high fees). Consequently, we introduced the idea of unbundling our estate planning services so that the corporate fiduciary would not be playing a controlling role. Rather, they would simply be playing one role in terms of the overall management of the client's trust. Simply stated, we would also have other individuals, called "trust protectors," involved in the management of the client's trust (i.e., a financial adviser who might be directing the client's finances); another adviser who might assist with the family dynamics involved in paying out benefits to the client's children, grandchildren, or other beneficiaries; and a tax preparer, outside of the trustee's office itself, who would be involved in some of the trust's income tax preparation. Essentially, we decided to take a more holistic approach to trust management, a big change from the way this practice was set up thirty years ago. Simply put, we wanted to make sure there was a process in place to ensure that the trustee could be held accountable for their actions, and that there could be a process for ensuring flexibility in relation to the trust.

Indeed, many clients have the misconception that once you set up a trust you cannot change it, and you are forever locked into a certain plan. In truth, there are many ways to create provisions, even within an irrevocable trust, with respect to giving trustees certain powers of appointment, and provisions that provide additional tax flexibility in terms of whether or when distributions are made. In many cases, the client does not realize how much flexibility is possible in these plans, and how much can be achieved simply by keeping property in trust rather than paying it out to a beneficiary at a certain age. There are also numerous creditor protections that can be put in place with respect to the repercussions from a messy divorce or bankruptcy. It is also important to consider the client's ability to pass wealth from one generation to the next indefinitely, due to the appeal against the rule of perpetuities in many states.

There has also been a misconception among many clients that avoiding probate at all costs is the main objective in estate planning. However, in states like Nebraska that have adopted the uniform probate code and do not even require a court appearance, probate actually offers some protections without really adding much expense. As one client recently observed, "Why would I want to fund my trust now and go through the cost of doing a pre-probate? Wouldn't it be cheaper to keep that money and administer probate at the appropriate time, because I expect to live a very long time?"

Daniel R. Stogsdill, a partner at Cline, Williams, Wright, Johnson & Oldfather LLP, is twenty-six-year veteran teacher and author for numerous university, law college, and financial planning courses. He has an "AV" listing in the Martindale-Hubbell Law Directory of Practicing Lawyers.

Mr. Stogsdill was a cadet at USMA-West Point from 1975 to 1976. He received his B.B.A. in international finance, with highest distinction, from the University of Hawaii in 1977 and his J.D., cum laude, from Indiana University in 1979.

Mr. Stogsdill is a member of the Lincoln, Nebraska and American Bar Associations, the National Academy of Elder Law Attorneys, and Attorneys for Family-Held Enterprises. He is admitted to the Nebraska Bar, the U.S. Supreme Court Bar, and the U.S. Tax Court Bar.

Preparing an Appropriate Strategy

Patricia Galteri

Chair of the Trusts & Estates Department

Meyer, Suozzi, English & Klein PC

ASPATORE

Thinking about Estate Planning for the First Time

People do not want to think about death and taxes, so it is not hard to understand that reluctant mindset. We advocate taking small steps (e.g., first a will, advance directives, an irrevocable life insurance trust, and so on), and as one ages so does the complexity of an estate plan.

Explain to a reluctant client that if you do not have a will, your state of domicile steps in and tells you how your assets will be distributed. Under the laws of intestacy, the client's estate may owe an estate tax that could have been avoided with proper planning. Intestacy often provides for distribution to people the client does not intend to benefit, or gives preference to the appointment of an administrator to an individual the client does not favor. These results motivate one to begin the process quickly. Asking questions about whether the client's family has sufficient liquidity to maintain the lifestyle it is accustomed to if the primary earner dies prematurely, and who the guardian of the minor children should be also help focus the client. Early on, the attorney should teach clients to engage in estate planning early in their lifetimes, as planned periodic lifetime gifting using the available exemption produces the best tax results.

The Client's Advisory Team

The team for most clients includes an attorney, accountant, insurance agent, and financial broker or their money manager. When working with a multifaceted team, it is important to have a point person to ensure there is clear communication and defined tasks. Sometimes the estate planning process lingers far too long because A thinks B is doing something, and B thinks C is taking care of that task. A point person can help ensure that all the team members are working collaboratively and efficiently for the benefit of the client.

The accountant is usually the person who has the requisite knowledge of the client's financial situation to recommend that he or she take action to mitigate the potential estate taxes. Either the accountant or a financial broker will recommend to the client to see an attorney who specializes in trusts and estates. The insurance adviser must be top-notch, familiar with the many rulings affecting arrangements involving life insurance. It is important that trustees of trusts that own life insurance also be counseled. Life insurance is an asset of the trust, an investment made by the trustee that must be continually monitored to avoid claims of imprudent investment or managing. A policy purchased ten years ago must be reviewed by the trustee to ensure it remains appropriate for the purposes it was purchased for, and to ensure it is performing well. The financial broker or money manager can assist us in determining performance of the assets placed in trusts such as a grantor-retained annuity trusts. To be successful, this total return of the trust must exceed the Internal Revenue Service's presumed rate of return. A financial broker can advise on how to create the grantor-retained annuity trusts, by sector or otherwise, and can assist in monitoring the performance. Knowing early on that the grantor-retained annuity trust might fail will allow us to revise the planning relative to that trust.

The First Client Meeting

The first meeting with a client is an ideal time to establish certain parameters that will determine whether we can work together. We spend an hour together (I do not charge for the time) getting to know each other and judging whether there is a foundation for a healthy working relationship.

If the clients are a married couple, it is considered a joint representation. It is very important that the clients understand that they are a client collectively. There can be no secrets. If we do a will one day, neither of them can return the next day and say they want to change it. Therefore, an engagement letter that spells out the terms of the joint representation is prepared so that there is no ambiguity. Our engagement letters for married couples follows that from the American College of Trust and Estate, and provides:

> **Joint Representation.** It is common for a husband and wife to engage the same attorney or law firm to assist in the planning of their estates. It is important for you to understand that since we will be representing both of you, you are considered our client, collectively. Accordingly, matters that one of you might discuss with us may be disclosed to the other of you. Ethical considerations

prohibit us from agreeing with either of you to withhold information from the other. In this matter, we will not give legal advice to either of you or make any changes in your estate planning documents without both parties' mutual knowledge and consent. Of course, anything either of you discusses with us is privileged from disclosure to third parties.

Conflict of Interest. If a conflict of interest arises between you during the course of your planning or if the two of you have a difference of opinion concerning the proposed plan for disposition of your property or any other issue, we can point out the pros and cons of your respective positions or differing opinions. However, ethical considerations once again prohibit us, as the attorneys for both of you, from advocating one of your positions over the other. Furthermore, we would not be able to advocate one of your positions versus the other if there is a dispute at any time as to your respective property rights or interests or as to other legal issues between you.

If actual conflicts of interest do arise between you of such a nature that in our judgment it is impossible for us to carry out our ethical obligations to both of you, it would become necessary for us to withdraw as attorneys for one or both of you. If we withdraw as attorneys for one of you, the other person would have to retain separate counsel to represent him or her.

If only one spouse meets with us initially, we will not proceed until we have a signed retainer letter from both and that we have an opportunity to review the discussions with the other spouse.

Working with Family Members

There are ethical challenges when working with family members during estate planning. Many times an elderly client may bring his or her child into a meeting. After explaining that the attorney-client privilege is waived, I ask the client whether he or she still wants the child to attend. As the attorney becomes intimately knowledgeable about the clients' family, counseling can become difficult when the children call upon you to encourage your clients (the parents) to take or not take certain courses of action. In the case of a family-run business, issues of control are prevalent. The cousins running the operations do not get along and vie for control, or siblings who want nothing to do with the day-to-day operation still want their fair share of the value, or if the business is promised to one child and the building used by the business is promised to another child, what has the parent accomplished? The situation can get messy, but the attorney must stay focused on the true client and the capacity in which you represent your client (e.g., individually, as a fiduciary, as an officer). If there is a real or perceived conflict, it must be identified and disclosed. Sometimes the clients can choose to waive the conflict in an appropriate writing. If, however, the conflict cannot be waived, you may have to disengage completely, even after several years of representation. That occurs when you realize you have so much personal business and financial information about each party that your representation would adversely affect the interests of another. Ultimately, the real challenge is getting to know the children of the client without causing conflicts of interest. They are the individuals who will select the attorneys handling their parents' estates, and if the children perceive you to provide value, it is likely you will be selected. The fact that you have represented their parents for twenty years does not guarantee an engagement with the children for their own estates.

Client-Driven Strategies

Clients often come to the table with a preconceived idea about how they want their estate structured. Their idea is not necessarily flawed, but you must examine the idea in the context of the applicable law and your client's motivations. Run the numbers and show the client the implications of their strategy under current law. Present alternatives using the client's plan, if possible, to demonstrate that there is value in considering a different approach. Often, when the client sees the numbers, they are receptive to a modification of a plan. If the existing plan is based on an irrevocable document, there are legal tools to revoke or modify instruments to revise a faulty or outdated plan.

Client strategies that seem off-target or misaligned with best practices are often based on common misconceptions. They believe that life insurance or jointly held property is non-taxable, or that use of revocable trusts avoids estate taxes, or that if there is no will the state will take their assets. Those misconceptions, combined with a lack of understanding about how to make tax-free gifts and how to use the exemptions, can result in bad strategy.

Patricia Galteri chairs Meyer, Suozzi, English & Klein PC's Trusts and Estates Department. Her practice includes the development of estate and business plans to ensure the transferring of wealth to the next generation, and she sees to the implementation of such plans through the drafting of wills, inter vivos trusts and testamentary trusts using the marital deduction, credit shelter, disclaimer and generation skipping provisions. She is well-versed with the use of lifetime trusts and other arrangements designed to transfer property at little or reduced gift tax cost to selected beneficiaries. Ms. Galteri supervises the preparation of probate and administration documents, provides advice in the marshaling and preservation of estate assets, and she is knowledgeable in all aspects of estate administration, post-mortem estate tax planning, and accounting issues. Ms. Galteri's department prepares federal and state estate tax returns and defends gift and estate tax audits. She is also called upon to appear in Surrogate's Court to participate in contested probate and accounting proceedings.

Ms. Galteri attended Hofstra University to earn a Bachelor's degree in business administration, emphasizing on accounting. She continued her studies at the Hofstra University School of Law and upon graduation, was presented with a Citation of Excellence in Community Law Service.

Ms. Galteri previously worked as a staff attorney in the tax department at one of the "Big Five" accounting firms in New York City, performing tax research for high net worth executives, multi-million dollar public and private companies, and restructured domestic corporations. She also participated in audits. Returning to Long Island, she worked as a tax consultant, primarily assisting in the preparation of business valuations in equitable distribution cases.

Ms. Galteri is rated "AV" by Martindale-Hubbell, the highest level in professional excellence and ethics. Her professional affiliations include membership in the New York State Bar Association, the Nassau County Bar Association, and the Suffolk County Bar Association. Ms. Galteri formerly chaired the Tax Committee of the Suffolk

County Bar Association, as well as the Bi-County Committee of Attorneys and Accountants. Currently, she is a member of the Nassau County Estate Planning Council and the North Shore-LIJ Health System's Gift Planning Advisory Committee. Ms. Galteri also serves on the Professional Advisory Committee of the Long Island Community Foundation.

ASPATORE